W....
2025 EDITION

THE INDIE AUTHOR ADVANTAGE: MASTERING CONTROL, ROYALTIES, AND REACH FOR SELF-PUBLISHING SUCCESS

Multi-Award-Winning-Author
B Alan Bourgeois

The Indie Author Advantage: Mastering Control, Royalties, and Reach for Self-Publishing Success

ISBN: 979-8-3484-0002-6

Publisher: Bourgeois Media & Consulting (BourgeoisMedia.com)

BOURGEOIS
MEDIA & CONSULTING

B ALAN BOUERGEOIS

STORYTELLING
LITERACY & HERITAGE

Thank you for purchasing this limited edition book, offered in celebration of the author's 50-year milestone. Proceeds from your purchase support the Texas Authors Institute of History, a museum founded by the author in 2015, dedicated to preserving the legacy of Texas authors.

https://TexasAuthors.Institute

The Indie Author Advantage

Dear Fellow Authors,

I'm delighted to introduce this book—and every guide in this series—as a short, easy-to-read resource designed to help you succeed in your writing journey. As writers, our true passion lies in creating stories, and I understand that delving into the business side of publishing might not be where we wish to spend most of our time.

That's why I've made a conscious effort to keep things simple and straightforward, focusing on practical advice without unnecessary fluff. You'll find that some concepts overlap between books, and that's intentional—to reinforce key ideas and ensure that whichever guide you pick up, you're equipped with valuable tools to enhance your success.

I genuinely hope you find these guides enjoyable and helpful. Your feedback means the world to me, and I look forward to hearing about your experiences and triumphs.

Happy writing, and here's to your continued success!

Introduction

Welcome to Your Indie Publishing Journey
Imagine this: a world where you, the author, hold the reins. Where your creative vision isn't compromised by a publishing house or delayed by endless red tape. Where the financial rewards of your hard work go straight to you, not through layers of intermediaries. That world exists—and it's called independent publishing.

The revolution of self-publishing has shattered traditional barriers, allowing authors from all walks of life to tell their stories, connect directly with readers, and reap the rewards of their efforts. Whether you're a debut author dreaming of seeing your name on a book cover, or a seasoned writer tired of traditional publishing's limitations, the indie path offers unprecedented opportunities.

This book is your guide to mastering independent publishing. We'll explore the practical tools and strategies you need to succeed—how to maintain creative control, maximize royalties, and market effectively. But more importantly, we'll show you how to embrace the freedom, flexibility, and satisfaction that come with being an indie author.

Here's what's inside:
- How to build a career as an independent author, step by step.
- The tools and platforms that will empower you to publish and distribute your books globally.
- Innovative marketing techniques tailored to indie authors.

The Indie Author Advantage

- Case studies of successful authors who have thrived on their terms.

By the end of this book, you'll have a complete understanding of the indie publishing process and the confidence to take charge of your writing career. Success is within your grasp, and it starts right here.

Contents

1
The Indie Author Advantage

Self-publishing is more than just skipping traditional gatekeepers—it's about embracing a philosophy of creative and professional freedom. Indie authors are trailblazers, taking risks and finding innovative ways to reach their audience. This chapter highlights the key advantages of independent publishing and how you can use them to your benefit.

1. Creative Freedom
One of the greatest joys of indie publishing is the ability to maintain total creative control. Every decision—plot twists, character arcs, cover design, marketing campaigns—rests in your hands.

> **Example**: Romance author Colleen Hoover achieved massive success by self-publishing novels that traditional publishers deemed too unconventional. Her unique style resonated deeply with readers, proving that following your vision pays off.

> **Action Tip**: Define your creative priorities early on. Do you have a specific vision for your book cover? A title you're determined to keep? Write down your non-negotiables before you begin the publishing process.

2. Higher Royalties
Traditional publishers typically offer royalties of 10–15% on book sales. In contrast, self-publishing platforms like Amazon KDP and Draft2Digital offer royalties as high as 70%. This financial difference can be life-changing, particularly for authors who build a loyal readership.

Case Study: Hugh Howey, the bestselling author of *Wool*, earned millions by self-publishing his sci-fi series. By retaining higher royalties and owning the rights to his work, Howey had the leverage to negotiate a lucrative print-only deal with a traditional publisher—while keeping his e-book earnings intact.

3. Faster Publishing Timeline

Traditional publishing often takes years to bring a book to market. Indie authors, however, can publish as soon as their book is ready. This agility allows you to respond quickly to trends or seasonal demand.

> **Example**: During the early months of the pandemic, indie authors who wrote escapist fiction capitalized on the demand for lighthearted stories by publishing quickly, often within weeks of completing their manuscripts.

4. Direct Access to Readers

Traditional authors often operate at a distance from their audience, relying on publishers to handle communication. Indie authors have the advantage of building direct relationships with their readers through social media, newsletters, and personal interactions.

> **Pro Tip**: Use platforms like Instagram and TikTok to connect with your readers. Share your writing journey, respond to comments, and involve your audience in the creative process.

5. Targeting Niche Markets

Mainstream publishers often avoid niche markets, prioritizing books with broad appeal. Indie authors can thrive by catering to specialized audiences.

> **Example**: Glynn Stewart found success by focusing on the niche market of space opera fans, a genre often overlooked by big publishers. By targeting this specific audience, he cultivated a loyal fanbase that eagerly anticipates each new release.

The Indie Author Advantage

2
Mastering Creative Control

One of the most liberating aspects of independent publishing is the ability to maintain complete creative control over your book. From the plot to the cover design, pricing, and marketing, every decision is yours to make. But with great power comes great responsibility. Exercising creative control effectively means balancing your vision with professional standards to ensure your work reaches its full potential.

The Power of Owning Your Vision

Creative control means having the freedom to tell your story exactly the way you envision it. Traditional publishers often push authors to modify their manuscripts to fit market trends, adjust content for broader appeal, or adopt titles and cover designs that align with their sales strategies. As an indie author, you are free to make decisions based on your goals and your readers' preferences.

> **Example**: Bestselling indie author Bella Andre built her career by writing contemporary romance novels with heartfelt and realistic storylines. Traditional publishers suggested changes to her stories to fit a more formulaic approach. By self-publishing, she stayed true to her vision, building a massive audience that resonated with her authenticity.

> **Pro Tip**: Define your creative priorities. Before diving into production, make a list of elements that are non-negotiable for you, whether it's your book's tone, title, or message. This clarity will guide your decisions as you proceed.

The Indie Author Advantage

The Role of Professional Standards
While creative freedom is invaluable, professional polish is essential. Indie authors must meet the same quality standards as traditionally published books to compete in the market. Readers expect compelling writing, professional editing, and visually appealing covers.

Editing Your Work
Editing is where great books are made. It's also one of the most common areas where indie authors cut corners. Avoid this trap—invest in high-quality editing to make your book the best it can be.

Types of Editing:
1. **Developmental Editing**: Focuses on structure, plot, pacing, and character development.
2. **Line Editing**: Refines sentence-level writing for clarity, style, and tone.
3. **Copyediting**: Checks grammar, punctuation, and consistency.
4. **Proofreading**: Provides a final polish to catch typos and formatting errors.

Tools to Explore: Grammarly and ProWritingAid can assist with self-editing, but professional human editors are irreplaceable for a polished manuscript.

Crafting a Standout Cover
Your cover is the first impression readers will have of your book. A professional, genre-appropriate cover can mean the difference between a potential reader clicking "Buy Now" or moving on to the next title.

> **Example**: Mystery author Mark Edwards attributes much of his success to his striking, suspenseful covers,

designed to match his genre's aesthetic. His consistent branding creates instant recognition among his fans.

Pro Tip: Use platforms like Reedsy or 99designs to find experienced book cover designers. Share a clear brief that includes your book's genre, tone, and target audience to ensure your cover resonates with readers.

Formatting for Professionalism

Proper formatting ensures your book looks polished, whether in print or digital format. Poor formatting can frustrate readers and lead to negative reviews.

Tools for Formatting:

- **Vellum** (Mac users): A user-friendly tool for creating beautifully formatted e-books and paperbacks.
- **Scrivener**: A versatile writing tool that also supports formatting.
- **Atticus**: A newer, multi-platform tool designed specifically for indie authors.

Balancing Creativity and Marketability

While staying true to your creative vision is important, remember that your book is also a product. Understanding your target audience and delivering a book that appeals to their preferences is key to success.

Researching Reader Expectations

- Study books in your genre to identify trends in cover design, pricing, and formatting.
- Read reviews of similar titles to learn what readers love—and what they don't.

Example: If you're writing fantasy, readers might expect richly detailed maps and epic, immersive cover art. Delivering on these expectations while maintaining your unique twist will help your book stand out in the market.

Case Study: Hugh Howey's Success with Creative Control

Hugh Howey's journey as an indie author exemplifies the power of creative control. His sci-fi series *Wool* was self-published, allowing him to experiment with pricing, serialization, and direct reader engagement. By retaining control of his work, Howey not only built a massive fanbase but also maintained ownership of his rights, leading to lucrative licensing deals while preserving his creative freedom.

Action Steps for Mastering Creative Control

1. **Prioritize Quality**: Invest in professional editing, cover design, and formatting.
2. **Define Your Vision**: Identify the core elements of your book that you're not willing to compromise on.
3. **Research the Market**: Learn what your target audience expects and find ways to meet those expectations without sacrificing your creativity.
4. **Collaborate with Professionals**: Hire skilled editors and designers to bring your vision to life.
5. **Create a Timeline**: Establish a realistic production schedule to ensure you have enough time to focus on each stage of the process.

Creative control is the cornerstone of indie publishing, but it's also a responsibility. By balancing your artistic vision with professional standards, you can create a book that stands out in the crowded marketplace and resonates with readers. In the next chapter, we'll explore one of the most exciting aspects of indie publishing: maximizing your royalties.

3
Maximizing Royalties

One of the most appealing aspects of independent publishing is the potential to earn significantly higher royalties than traditionally published authors. While traditional publishers typically offer 10–15% royalties on book sales, self-publishing platforms like Amazon Kindle Direct Publishing (KDP), Draft2Digital, and IngramSpark allow authors to retain up to 70–80% of their earnings. However, maximizing your royalties requires strategic decisions about pricing, distribution, and additional revenue streams.

This chapter will equip you with the tools and insights to take full advantage of the financial opportunities available to indie authors.

Understanding Royalty Rates
Royalty rates vary based on the platform, format, and pricing of your book. Here's a breakdown of what you can expect from the major platforms:
- **Amazon KDP (E-books)**: Authors earn 70% royalties on books priced between $2.99 and $9.99. For books outside this range, royalties drop to 35%.
- **Amazon KDP (Print-on-Demand)**: Royalties for paperbacks depend on the book's price and printing costs. Authors generally keep around 60% of the list price after deducting printing expenses.
- **Draft2Digital and Smashwords**: Both offer wide distribution to platforms like Apple Books, Barnes & Noble, and Kobo, with royalties typically around 60%.

The Indie Author Advantage

- **IngramSpark**: Ideal for authors looking to distribute to brick-and-mortar bookstores, though royalties tend to be lower due to distribution fees.

Setting the Right Price

Pricing is a critical factor in determining how much you'll earn—and how many readers will purchase your book. Too high, and you risk alienating potential buyers; too low, and you may undervalue your work.

The Sweet Spot for E-books

For e-books, $2.99 to $4.99 is often the ideal range. It's affordable enough to attract readers while keeping you within the 70% royalty bracket on platforms like Amazon.

> **Example**: An author selling an e-book for $4.99 with 70% royalties will earn approximately $3.50 per sale. Compare this to a $0.99 book, which only brings in about $0.35 at 35% royalties.

Pricing for Print Books

Print books are often priced higher than e-books to cover printing costs while maintaining profitability. Research books in your genre to find a competitive yet appealing price point.

> **Pro Tip**: Use online tools like Amazon's *Printing Cost Calculator* to determine the profit margin for your paperback or hardcover.

Leveraging Multiple Revenue Streams

Maximizing royalties isn't just about selling e-books. Indie authors have several options to diversify their income:

1. Audiobooks

The audiobook market is booming, with platforms like Audible, ACX, and Findaway Voices offering indie authors a way to reach a growing audience of listeners. Audiobooks typically yield higher price points and royalties.

> **Example**: An indie thriller author prices their audiobook at $19.99, earning $7–$8 per sale depending on the

platform. With audiobooks becoming increasingly popular, this format can generate substantial income.

Pro Tip: If you're on a budget, consider narrating your audiobook yourself, provided you have the right equipment and a clear, engaging voice.

2. Print-on-Demand (POD)

Platforms like Amazon KDP Print and IngramSpark allow you to sell paperback and hardcover editions without investing in inventory. Print books also cater to readers who prefer physical copies, expanding your audience.

> **Action Step**: Offer both a standard paperback edition and a premium hardcover edition for dedicated fans willing to pay more for a high-quality product.

3. Foreign Language Editions

If your book gains traction, translating it into other languages can open up international markets. Platforms like Babelcube and Reedsy offer translation services, while global distribution channels like Tolino help you reach readers in Europe and beyond.

> **Example**: Joanna Penn translated her non-fiction books into multiple languages, significantly increasing her reach and royalties from international markets.

Exclusive vs. Wide Distribution

One key decision indie authors face is whether to enroll in Amazon's **KDP Select** program, which offers benefits like Kindle Unlimited royalties and promotional tools, or to go wide by distributing across multiple platforms.

Benefits of KDP Select (Exclusive)

- Earn royalties from Kindle Unlimited and Kindle Owners' Lending Library reads.
- Access promotional tools like free book days and Kindle Countdown Deals.

The Indie Author Advantage

Consider This: Enrolling in KDP Select means your e-book is exclusive to Amazon, limiting your reach to other platforms like Apple Books or Kobo.

Benefits of Wide Distribution
- Access readers across multiple platforms and countries.
- Diversify your income, reducing reliance on Amazon.

Pro Tip: Start with KDP Select for the first 90 days to build traction and reviews, then switch to wide distribution to expand your audience.

Case Study: Mark Dawson's Income Strategy
Mark Dawson, a bestselling indie thriller author, exemplifies how to maximize royalties through strategic pricing and diverse revenue streams. By pricing his e-books competitively, producing audiobooks, and offering both print and digital editions, Dawson earns a six-figure annual income. He also runs targeted advertising campaigns to boost visibility and drive sales.

The Role of Promotions in Boosting Royalties
Promotions can significantly impact your book's visibility and sales, leading to higher royalties over time. Here are a few strategies to consider:

Free and Discounted Book Promotions
Offering your book for free or at a steep discount for a limited time can generate downloads, build reviews, and attract new readers to your catalog.

Example: If you have a series, make the first book free to hook readers and encourage them to buy the sequels.

Email Newsletter Promotions
Promotional sites like BookBub, Freebooksy, and Bargain Booksy send your discounted or free book to their massive subscriber lists, often leading to hundreds or thousands of downloads.

Action Step: Research promotional sites and plan your campaigns strategically. For example, combine a BookBub feature with an Amazon Countdown Deal for maximum impact.

Action Steps for Maximizing Royalties
1. **Research Pricing**: Study successful books in your genre to identify optimal price points.
2. **Diversify Formats**: Offer your book as an e-book, paperback, and audiobook.
3. **Experiment with Promotions**: Use free and discounted promotions to boost visibility and long-term sales.
4. **Consider Global Markets**: Translate your work to reach international readers.
5. **Monitor and Adjust**: Use analytics from platforms like Amazon KDP and Book Report to track sales and refine your strategies.

Maximizing royalties as an indie author is about more than just choosing the right platform—it's about thinking strategically, diversifying your offerings, and always keeping your readers in mind. In the next chapter, we'll explore how to target niche markets effectively and turn your unique perspective into a competitive advantage.

4
Targeting Niche Markets

One of the greatest advantages of self-publishing is the ability to reach niche markets. Unlike traditional publishers, who focus on broad, mainstream audiences, indie authors can connect with specific reader communities. Whether it's a unique genre, a highly targeted demographic, or a specialized topic, niche markets offer a world of opportunity for authors who know how to reach them.

In this chapter, we'll explore how to identify your niche, build a connection with your target audience, and create a book that resonates deeply with your readers.

Why Niche Markets Matter

Traditional publishers often avoid niche topics because they perceive the potential audience as too small to justify the investment. However, indie authors can thrive in these markets because:

- Niche readers are often more loyal and passionate.
- There's less competition compared to mainstream genres.
- You can target your marketing efforts more precisely, reducing costs and increasing effectiveness.

Example: Cozy mysteries featuring baking themes are a thriving subgenre. Authors like Joanne Fluke, who write about amateur sleuths with a love of cooking, attract devoted readers who seek stories that combine mystery and culinary elements.

Pro Tip: Niche markets don't mean small profits. Even a relatively small, loyal audience can generate significant income over time.

How to Identify Your Niche
The first step in targeting a niche market is understanding what makes your work unique. Here are some questions to guide you:
1. **What themes or genres do you love?** Passion is key to writing authentically and connecting with your audience.
2. **What specific audience would appreciate your book?** Think beyond broad genres like "romance" or "fantasy." Are you writing romance featuring older protagonists? Fantasy with an eco-conscious twist?
3. **What gaps exist in the market?** Research your genre on platforms like Amazon and Goodreads. Look for underserved subgenres or unmet reader expectations.

Research Tools for Niche Discovery
- **Amazon Categories**: Explore the subcategories in your genre to identify specific niches.
- **Goodreads**: Read reviews of similar books to understand what readers love and what they want more of.
- **Reader Communities**: Join Reddit groups, Facebook communities, and online forums related to your niche.

Example: An author writing steampunk novels notices a lack of diverse representation in the genre. By creating a steampunk series with multicultural characters, they tap into an underserved market and attract enthusiastic readers.

Building a Reader Persona
A reader persona is a detailed profile of your ideal reader. It helps you understand their needs, preferences, and habits, allowing you to tailor your writing and marketing effectively.

The Indie Author Advantage

How to Create a Reader Persona
1. **Demographics**: Age, gender, location, education level.
2. **Interests**: What hobbies or passions align with your niche? (e.g., cat lovers, history buffs).
3. **Buying Habits**: Do they prefer e-books, audiobooks, or print? How much are they willing to spend?
4. **Pain Points**: What problem does your book solve, or what emotional experience does it deliver?

Example Persona:
- Name: Sarah
- Age: 35
- Interests: Cozy mysteries, baking, cats
- Preferred Format: E-books under $5
- Pain Point: Wants lighthearted, comforting stories to unwind after work

Writing for Your Niche
Tailor your story to meet the expectations of your niche while still bringing your unique voice to the table.

> **Example**: If your niche is historical romance, research the time period extensively to create a setting that feels authentic. Include historically accurate details while weaving a compelling love story that resonates emotionally.

Balancing Authenticity and Creativity
While it's important to meet reader expectations, don't be afraid to innovate. A fresh twist can set your book apart.

> **Example**: Paranormal romance author Nalini Singh blended traditional romantic tropes with complex world-building and unique supernatural elements, carving out a loyal following in her niche.

Marketing to Niche Audiences
Once you've identified your niche and written a book tailored to your readers, the next step is connecting with your audience. Here are some proven strategies:

1. Social Media
Use platforms like Facebook, Instagram, and TikTok to engage with niche communities. Share content that reflects your book's themes, such as behind-the-scenes writing insights, character profiles, or fun facts related to your niche.

> **Example**: A steampunk author might share images of Victorian-era inventions or host live Q&A sessions about world-building.

2. Content Marketing
Create valuable content that draws your target audience. Blog posts, videos, and podcasts are great ways to showcase your expertise and build trust.

> **Example**: A non-fiction author writing about vegan cooking for athletes could share recipes, workout tips, and meal plans on their blog to attract their ideal readers.

3. Niche Advertising
Platforms like Amazon Ads and Facebook Ads allow you to target specific demographics and interests. Focus your campaigns on keywords and phrases that align with your niche.

> **Action Tip**: If you're writing medieval fantasy, target readers who have purchased books by authors like George R.R. Martin or J.R.R. Tolkien.

4. Collaborations
Partner with influencers, bloggers, and other authors in your niche. Joint promotions, giveaways, and blog tours can significantly increase your visibility.

> **Example**: Cozy mystery authors might collaborate on a holiday-themed anthology, cross-promoting to their combined fanbases.

> **Case Study: Lindsay Buroker's Fantasy Success**
> Lindsay Buroker, an indie author specializing in fantasy and steampunk, built a thriving career by focusing on

niche audiences. She connected with readers through blog posts, social media, and a consistent release schedule, earning a loyal following that drives strong sales for every new release.

Action Steps for Targeting Niche Markets
1. **Define Your Niche**: Identify your unique angle and audience.
2. **Create a Reader Persona**: Understand your ideal reader's habits, interests, and pain points.
3. **Engage with Communities**: Join forums, groups, and discussions related to your niche.
4. **Experiment with Marketing**: Test different platforms and campaigns to find what resonates with your audience.
5. **Stay Consistent**: Build trust by delivering high-quality books that meet your readers' expectations.

Niche markets offer indie authors an incredible opportunity to stand out and build lasting connections with their readers. In the next chapter, we'll dive into how you can build a personal brand that amplifies your success and makes you unforgettable to your audience.

5
Building a Personal Brand

In the competitive world of indie publishing, your personal brand is your greatest asset. It's what sets you apart from other authors, creates trust with your readers, and builds long-term loyalty. A strong personal brand helps readers recognize your work, understand what you stand for, and connect with you on a deeper level.

This chapter will guide you through the process of crafting and maintaining a personal brand that resonates with your audience and amplifies your success as an indie author.

What Is a Personal Brand?
Your personal brand is the unique identity you cultivate as an author. It encompasses:
1. **Your Voice**: The tone and style of your writing and public communication.
2. **Your Message**: The themes, values, and ideas your work represents.
3. **Your Presence**: How you present yourself on social media, your website, and at events.

Example: Joanna Penn, author and host of *The Creative Penn* podcast, has built a personal brand around her expertise in self-publishing and her passion for helping other authors succeed. Her brand reflects professionalism, innovation, and encouragement.

The Importance of Branding for Indie Authors
A strong personal brand offers several key benefits:
1. **Reader Recognition**: Readers know what to expect from you and your books.

2. **Emotional Connection**: A relatable brand fosters loyalty and trust.
3. **Marketing Power**: A recognizable brand makes it easier to market new releases and grow your audience.
4. **Long-Term Growth**: Your brand evolves with you, allowing you to expand into new genres or mediums while keeping your audience engaged.

Example: Romance author Colleen Hoover started with self-published contemporary romance novels and transitioned to more complex literary fiction while maintaining her brand's emotional authenticity.

How to Define Your Personal Brand
1. Identify Your Unique Voice
What makes you different from other authors in your genre? Your voice should reflect your personality and writing style.

> **Exercise**: Write down three words that describe your writing style (e.g., witty, heartfelt, dark). These words will serve as the foundation of your brand.

2. Clarify Your Message
What do you want readers to associate with your work? Your message could be tied to the themes you explore, the emotions you evoke, or the problems you solve.

> **Example**: If you write motivational non-fiction, your message might be: "Empowering readers to take control of their lives and achieve their goals."

3. Understand Your Audience
Who are you writing for? Your personal brand should resonate with your ideal reader. Use the reader persona you developed in Chapter 4 to guide your branding decisions.

> **Action Step**: Create content that speaks directly to your audience's needs and interests. For instance, if your audience loves fantasy with strong female leads, share insights about your characters and world-building.

Building Your Brand Platform
Once you've defined your personal brand, it's time to communicate it effectively across various platforms.

1. Your Author Website
Your website is the hub of your personal brand. It should be professional, visually appealing, and easy to navigate. Include:
- **An Author Bio**: Share your journey, values, and inspiration.
- **Your Books**: Display your work with clear descriptions, links to purchase, and sample chapters.
- **A Blog or News Section**: Engage readers with updates, behind-the-scenes content, or related topics.
- **A Mailing List Signup**: Build your email list by offering a freebie (e.g., a short story, checklist, or excerpt).

Pro Tip: Use tools like Squarespace, Wix, or WordPress to create a polished website without needing advanced technical skills.

2. Social Media Presence
Social media platforms like Instagram, TikTok, Twitter, and Facebook are essential tools for building your personal brand. Choose platforms that align with your audience and brand identity.

Examples:
- **TikTok (BookTok)**: Share short, engaging videos about your writing process, book recommendations, or funny moments related to your genre.
- **Instagram**: Post visually appealing content like cover reveals, fan art, or photos of your writing space.
- **Twitter**: Engage in conversations about topics relevant to your niche or genre.

The Indie Author Advantage

> **Pro Tip**: Be authentic. Readers connect more with authors who share their personalities, struggles, and triumphs.

3. Your Mailing List

An email list is one of the most valuable assets for indie authors. Unlike social media, you own your mailing list, and it provides a direct line of communication with your readers'

Action Steps:

1. Offer an incentive for signing up (e.g., a free short story, a sneak peek of your next book).
2. Send regular newsletters with updates, exclusive content, and special offers.
3. Use tools like MailerLite or ConvertKit to manage your email list.

4. Visual Branding

Your visuals—book covers, social media graphics, website design—should align with your brand identity.

> **Example**: An indie horror author might use dark, eerie imagery with bold fonts, while a romance author might opt for pastel colors and soft, romantic typography.

Engaging with Your Audience

Engagement is the key to building a loyal reader base. Readers want to feel connected to you as a person, not just an author.

1. Share Your Journey

Let readers in on your writing process, from brainstorming to final edits. Share your triumphs, challenges, and lessons learned.

> **Example**: Fantasy author Brandon Sanderson regularly updates fans about his progress on new projects, creating anticipation and fostering trust.

2. Interact Authentically
Respond to comments, messages, and reviews. Readers appreciate authors who take the time to engage with them.

3. Host Events and Giveaways
Virtual events, such as live Q&A sessions or book club discussions, can help you connect with your audience. Giveaways are also a great way to reward loyal readers and attract new ones.

> **Example**: An author celebrating a book launch could host a giveaway for signed copies or exclusive swag.

> ### Case Study: Penny Reid's Brand of Connection
> Penny Reid, a bestselling romance author, has built a brand centered on humor, relatability, and authentic engagement. By sharing personal anecdotes and interacting with her readers on social media, she has cultivated a devoted fanbase that eagerly anticipates her new releases.

Action Steps for Building Your Personal Brand
1. **Define Your Brand**: Identify your unique voice, message, and audience.
2. **Create a Website**: Develop a professional author site with clear branding.
3. **Choose Your Platforms**: Focus on social media channels that align with your audience.
4. **Engage Regularly**: Share updates, respond to readers, and host events.
5. **Stay Consistent**: Ensure your brand is cohesive across all platforms and materials.

Your personal brand is the bridge between you and your readers. By building a strong, authentic brand, you'll not only attract more readers but also deepen your connection with them. In the next chapter, we'll explore innovative marketing strategies to amplify your reach and drive book sales.

The Indie Author Advantage

6
Innovative Marketing Strategies

Marketing is the lifeblood of your indie publishing career. You've written an amazing book and built a strong personal brand— now it's time to get your work in front of readers. The beauty of self-publishing is the flexibility it offers: you can experiment, adapt, and find what works best for your audience. In this chapter, we'll explore innovative marketing strategies that go beyond the basics to help you connect with readers, increase visibility, and drive sales.

The Foundations of Effective Marketing

Before diving into specific strategies, it's essential to understand the key principles of successful marketing:

1. **Know Your Audience**: The better you understand your readers, the more targeted and effective your marketing will be.
2. **Be Consistent**: Consistency in messaging, visuals, and outreach builds trust and recognition.
3. **Engage, Don't Sell**: Modern marketing is about building relationships, not hard-selling. Focus on creating value for your audience.

Pro Tip: Establish clear goals for your marketing efforts, whether it's growing your email list, boosting sales for a new release, or increasing social media engagement.

Social Media Marketing

Social media is a powerful tool for reaching readers and building relationships. Each platform offers unique opportunities— choose the ones that align with your strengths and audience.

4. TikTok (BookTok)

TikTok has become a hotspot for book promotion, with millions of readers discovering new titles through short, engaging videos.

Content Ideas:
- Show behind-the-scenes glimpses of your writing process.
- Share "aesthetic" videos that match your book's mood or theme.
- Use trending hashtags like #BookTok and #IndieAuthor to increase visibility.

Example: Romance author Tessa Bailey gained significant traction by sharing TikTok videos that showcased her book covers and humorous scenes, engaging directly with fans.

2. Instagram

Instagram's visual nature makes it ideal for authors who want to showcase their books and connect with readers.

What to Post:
- High-quality images of your book covers, writing setup, or fan art.
- Short videos or Reels featuring writing tips or character inspiration.
- Stories with interactive polls or Q&A sessions to engage your audience.

5. Facebook Groups

Facebook groups remain a goldmine for niche audiences. Join or create groups that cater to your genre or themes.

> **Action Step**: Start a private group for your readers. Offer exclusive content like early access to chapters, giveaways, or live discussions.

Email Marketing

An email list is one of the most reliable ways to reach your readers. Unlike social media, where algorithms control visibility, email ensures your message lands directly in your audience's inbox.

Building Your List

- Offer a freebie, such as a novella or a checklist, in exchange for signups.
- Promote your email list on your website, social media, and in your books.

What to Include in Your Newsletters

- Updates on your writing progress and upcoming releases.
- Exclusive excerpts or sneak peeks.
- Personal stories or reflections to build rapport.

Example: Author Lindsay Buroker uses her email list to keep fans engaged by sharing updates, asking for feedback, and announcing new releases. Her personal approach fosters loyalty and consistent sales.

Book Promotions

Running promotions is a fantastic way to boost visibility, especially for new releases or when launching a series.

1. Free and Discounted Promotions

Offering your book for free or at a reduced price can generate downloads and reviews, which improve your book's ranking on platforms like Amazon.

> **Action Step**: Combine a free book promotion with advertising on sites like BookBub, Freebooksy, or Bargain Booksy for maximum exposure.

The Indie Author Advantage

2. Series Launch Strategies
If you're launching a series, price the first book lower (or make it free) to entice readers into the series. Once they're hooked, they'll purchase subsequent books.
Example: Author Bella Forrest built her career by releasing her *A Shade of Vampire* series with a low entry price point, encouraging readers to binge the entire series.

Leveraging Paid Advertising
Paid ads can amplify your reach, but they require careful planning and monitoring to be effective.

1. Amazon Ads
Amazon Ads allow you to target readers by keywords, categories, or even similar authors. Start small with a modest budget and test different campaigns to find what works.
> **Pro Tip**: Use Amazon's "Sponsored Products" option to showcase your book directly on the pages of similar titles.

2. Facebook Ads
Facebook's advanced targeting tools let you reach specific demographics and interests.
> **Action Step**: Experiment with ad copy, visuals, and audience targeting. Monitor your ad performance and adjust based on what drives the best results.

Collaborations and Community Engagement
Collaborating with other authors and engaging with the reader community can significantly boost your visibility.

1. Collaborate with Authors
Join forces with authors in your genre for cross-promotions, anthology projects, or joint giveaways. By pooling your audiences, everyone benefits.

Example: A group of cozy mystery authors might collaborate on a themed anthology, promoting it to their combined fanbases.

2. Attend Virtual Events
Participate in online book festivals, webinars, or virtual readings to connect with readers and fellow authors.

Action Step: Host a live event to celebrate a book launch, complete with a reading, Q&A, and giveaways.

Innovative Approaches to Marketing
In addition to the strategies above, consider trying out creative and unconventional marketing ideas to stand out.

1. Create a Podcast or YouTube Channel
Sharing content about your genre, writing tips, or the publishing process can help you build an audience beyond your books.

Example: Joanna Penn's *The Creative Penn* podcast has not only grown her readership but also established her as a leading voice in self-publishing.

2. Crowdfunding Campaigns
Platforms like Kickstarter and Patreon allow you to raise funds for your projects while engaging directly with fans. Offer rewards like signed copies, exclusive merchandise, or early access to your books.

Example: Author Michael J. Sullivan funded his books through Kickstarter, building excitement and raising thousands of dollars before publication.

Case Study: How Mark Dawson Built a Marketing Empire
Mark Dawson, author of the *John Milton* thriller series, is a master of indie marketing. By combining email marketing, paid advertising, and consistent reader engagement, Dawson has built a six-figure career. He

also shares his expertise through courses that have helped thousands of indie authors succeed.

Action Steps for Marketing Your Book

1. **Choose Your Platforms**: Focus on the social media platforms where your audience spends the most time.
2. **Build Your List**: Start growing your email list immediately—it's your most reliable marketing tool.
3. **Experiment with Ads**: Test Amazon and Facebook ads to find the right audience and messaging.
4. **Collaborate Creatively**: Partner with other authors or influencers to expand your reach.
5. **Stay Consistent**: Marketing is a marathon, not a sprint. Regularly engage with your audience and refine your strategies over time.

Marketing is a dynamic process that evolves with your career. By staying creative, consistent, and reader-focused, you'll not only increase your book sales but also build a loyal following that supports you for years to come. In the next chapter, we'll dive into the power of community support and how collaboration can elevate your indie author journey.

7
Community Support

Self-publishing can feel like a solitary endeavor at times, but one of the most empowering aspects of being an indie author is the strength of the community. Independent authors often band together to share resources, offer encouragement, and collaborate in ways that elevate everyone involved. The indie author community is built on a spirit of support and collaboration, making it a valuable resource for both newcomers and veterans.

In this chapter, we'll explore how to build and leverage your connections within the indie author community, participate in collaborative efforts, and harness the power of mutual support to achieve success.

Why Community Support Matters

Unlike the traditional publishing world, where authors often compete for limited opportunities, the indie publishing community thrives on shared success. Here's why community support is essential:

- **Shared Knowledge**: Access to insights and experiences from other authors can help you avoid mistakes and accelerate your progress.
- **Collaboration Opportunities**: Working with others allows you to expand your reach and tackle projects you couldn't do alone.
- **Emotional Support**: Writing and publishing can be challenging. Having a network of peers who understand your struggles can make the journey less daunting.

Pro Tip: Think of the indie author community as a team, not competition. When one author succeeds, it benefits the entire community by raising the profile of independent publishing as a whole.

How to Connect with Other Authors

Building relationships with fellow indie authors is easier than ever, thanks to online tools and social media. Here's where to start:

1. Join Online Communities

Platforms like Facebook, Reddit, and Discord host thriving groups where authors share advice, discuss trends, and provide feedback.

Recommended Groups:
- **20BooksTo50K**: A popular Facebook group focused on helping authors achieve financial independence through self-publishing.
- **Self-Publishing Subreddit**: A helpful forum for discussing every aspect of indie publishing.
- **Writing Discord Servers**: Many Discord communities host live chats and workshops for writers.

Action Step: Join at least two communities and introduce yourself. Share your goals and offer to help others—it's a great way to build relationships.

2. Attend Conferences and Webinars

Indie author conferences and virtual events provide opportunities to learn from experts, network with peers, and discover new tools and strategies.

Examples:
- **Self-Publishing Show Live**: A conference hosted by Mark Dawson that covers marketing, publishing, and more.
- **Writer's Digest Conferences**: Regular events featuring panels, workshops, and networking sessions.

Pro Tip: If in-person events aren't feasible, webinars and virtual summits are just as valuable. Take advantage of opportunities to interact with panelists and attendees.

3. Build Genuine Relationships
Networking isn't just about collecting contacts—it's about creating meaningful connections. Be authentic, supportive, and willing to contribute to the success of others.

> **Example**: Fantasy author Lindsay Buroker often shares her marketing strategies and experiences with other authors. This generosity has helped her build a loyal network of peers who support her work in return.

Collaboration Opportunities
Collaborating with other indie authors can significantly boost your visibility and income. Here are some ways to team up:

1. Anthologies
Participating in or organizing an anthology is a great way to reach new readers. Each author brings their audience to the table, creating a win-win for everyone involved.

> **Example**: A group of romance authors creates a holiday-themed anthology. Each author contributes a short story, and the anthology is marketed to their combined fanbases, resulting in increased exposure for all.

2. Cross-Promotion
Authors in the same genre can promote each other's books through newsletters, social media, and blog posts.

> **Action Step**: Identify authors in your niche and propose a cross-promotion campaign. For example, you could offer to feature their book in your newsletter in exchange for them doing the same.

3. Co-Authoring
Co-authoring a book with another writer allows you to combine your strengths and share the workload. It also gives you access to each other's audiences.

> **Example**: Science fiction authors Jay Kristoff and Amie Kaufman co-wrote *The Illuminae Files*, blending their unique styles into a hit series that attracted fans of both authors.

Giving Back to the Community
A strong community thrives on mutual support. As you benefit from the indie author network, consider how you can contribute in return.

1. Share Your Knowledge
Whether it's through blog posts, social media tips, or speaking at events, sharing your experiences helps other authors succeed.

> **Example**: Joanna Penn built her brand not only by publishing her own books but also by creating a podcast and blog to share insights about writing and self-publishing.

2. Offer Feedback
Provide constructive feedback on other authors' work or marketing strategies. This builds goodwill and strengthens your connections.

3. Celebrate Others' Success
Cheer for your fellow authors' achievements, big or small. Their success doesn't diminish yours—in fact, it strengthens the indie community as a whole.

> **Case Study: The Power of Community in Anthologies**
> The *Romance for Hope* anthology brought together a group of indie romance authors to raise funds for charity. Each author contributed a story, and the anthology was marketed collaboratively. The project not only raised

significant funds but also introduced readers to new authors, showcasing the potential of community-driven efforts.

Action Steps for Building Community Support

1. **Join Groups**: Find at least two online communities to participate in regularly.
2. **Attend Events**: Sign up for a conference or webinar to learn and network.
3. **Collaborate**: Reach out to other authors for anthologies, cross-promotions, or co-authoring opportunities.
4. **Give Back**: Share your insights and celebrate the successes of others to strengthen the community.
5. **Build Relationships**: Engage authentically with peers, offering support and encouragement.

By embracing the power of community, you'll not only grow your career but also contribute to a supportive ecosystem that benefits all indie authors. In the next chapter, we'll explore how adaptability can help you thrive in the ever-changing landscape of self-publishing.

8
Adaptability

The publishing industry is constantly evolving. Trends come and go, platforms change their algorithms, and reader expectations shift. For indie authors, adaptability is not just a helpful trait—it's a necessity. By staying flexible and open to change, you can navigate challenges, seize new opportunities, and keep your career thriving.

This chapter will explore how to cultivate adaptability, respond to changes in the market, and future-proof your writing career.

Why Adaptability Matters

The indie publishing world offers a wealth of opportunities, but it's also unpredictable. The strategies that work today may not work tomorrow. Being adaptable allows you to:

- **Stay Relevant**: Respond to new trends and technologies that capture readers' attention.
- **Improve Your Work**: Incorporate feedback and evolve as a writer to meet changing reader expectations.
- **Expand Your Reach**: Explore new platforms, genres, or formats to grow your audience.

Example: When TikTok's #BookTok community exploded in popularity, many indie authors pivoted their marketing strategies to include short, engaging videos. Authors who embraced the platform saw dramatic increases in sales.

Embracing Change

Adapting to change starts with a mindset shift. Instead of viewing changes as obstacles, see them as opportunities to innovate and grow.

1. Monitor Industry Trends
Stay informed about changes in the publishing world. Follow blogs, listen to podcasts, and participate in author forums to keep your finger on the pulse.

Recommended Resources:
- *The Creative Penn Podcast* (Joanna Penn)
- *Self-Publishing Show* (Mark Dawson)
- Industry news sites like *Publishers Weekly* and *Jane Friedman's Blog*.

2. Experiment with New Platforms
When new tools or platforms emerge, don't be afraid to test them. Early adopters often have a competitive advantage.
> **Example**: Bella Andre was one of the first indie authors to embrace print-on-demand services, allowing her to offer paperbacks to fans while keeping costs low.

Pro Tip: Dedicate a small portion of your time or budget to experimenting with new marketing strategies or platforms. If something doesn't work, treat it as a learning experience.

Adapting Your Writing Process
Adaptability isn't just about marketing—it's also about your craft. As reader preferences evolve, so should your writing.
1. Responding to Reader Feedback
Your readers are your most valuable source of insight. Pay attention to reviews, emails, and social media comments to understand what they love—and what they don't.
> **Action Step**: After releasing a book, analyze its reception. Did readers enjoy the pacing? Were there complaints about unresolved plot points? Use this feedback to improve your next project.

2. Exploring New Genres

If your current genre feels saturated or sales are declining, consider branching out. Writing in a new genre can reinvigorate your creativity and attract a fresh audience.

Example: Romance author Kristen Ashley transitioned to romantic suspense, successfully expanding her readership while staying true to her brand.

3. Experimenting with Formats

Adapt your work to meet the growing demand for audiobooks, serialized fiction, or even graphic novels.

> **Case Study**: Michael Anderle, creator of the *Kurtherian Gambit* series, used serialized releases to build a massive following. By releasing shorter, episodic stories, he kept readers engaged and eager for the next installment.

Future-Proofing Your Career

While adaptability is about responding to immediate changes, future-proofing ensures long-term success. Here's how to build a career that can withstand industry shifts:

4. Build Direct Relationships with Readers

Social media algorithms and platform policies can change overnight, but your email list is yours to control. Focus on growing and nurturing your mailing list.

> **Action Step**: Regularly communicate with your subscribers through newsletters. Share updates, offer exclusive content, and maintain a personal connection.

5. Diversify Your Revenue Streams

Relying on a single platform or format makes your income vulnerable to changes. Diversify by:

- Selling on multiple platforms (e.g., Amazon, Kobo, Apple Books).
- Offering audiobooks, print-on-demand, and special editions.

- Licensing your work for translations or adaptations.

Example: Joanna Penn expanded her income by selling foreign rights and offering online courses for writers, creating a stable and diversified revenue base.

6. Develop a Long-Term Vision

Think about where you want your writing career to be in five or ten years. Set goals that align with your values and build toward them steadily.

> **Pro Tip**: Keep a "growth mindset." Even if something doesn't work as planned, focus on what you learned and how you can apply that knowledge moving forward.

Case Study: Lindsay Buroker's Adaptability

Fantasy and steampunk author Lindsay Buroker exemplifies adaptability. When sales for her early books slowed, she experimented with new genres, pricing models, and marketing tactics. Her willingness to pivot and try new approaches helped her build a sustainable career, with consistent releases and a loyal fanbase.

Action Steps for Cultivating Adaptability

- **Stay Curious**: Commit to learning about new tools, trends, and strategies.
- **Experiment Regularly**: Dedicate time to testing new ideas, from marketing platforms to writing techniques.
- **Gather Feedback**: Listen to your readers and peers to identify areas for improvement.
- **Diversify Income**: Explore multiple formats, platforms, and markets to create a stable career.
- **Focus on Growth**: Treat setbacks as opportunities to learn and evolve.

Adaptability is the hallmark of a successful indie author. By staying flexible, open-minded, and proactive, you can not only survive the ever-changing landscape of publishing but thrive in it. In the next chapter, we'll explore the deep sense of personal

The Indie Author Advantage

satisfaction that comes from crafting a career on your own terms.

9
Personal Satisfaction

Independent publishing isn't just a business or a creative endeavor—it's a deeply fulfilling journey. As an indie author, you have the power to shape your career, share your stories with the world, and connect with readers in meaningful ways. This chapter explores the unique sense of personal satisfaction that comes from self-publishing and how embracing this fulfillment can fuel your long-term success.

The Joy   reateion

At its core, writing is an act of creation. You're taking ideas from your imagination and transforming them into something tangible—a book that readers can hold, enjoy, and cherish. This process is inherently rewarding.

7. Freedom to Write What You Love

Unlike traditional publishing, where market trends often dictate the content, indie publishing allows you to write the stories you're passionate about.

> **Example**: Science fiction author Hugh Howey initially self-published *Wool* as a series of novellas, ignoring traditional publishers' advice to write a standalone novel. Staying true to his vision paid off, as his work resonated deeply with readers.

8. Seeing Your Book in the World

There's nothing quite like the moment you hold your finished book in your hands or see it listed on a platform like Amazon. That feeling of accomplishment is a testament to your hard work and perseverance.

Pro Tip: Celebrate each milestone, whether it's finishing your first draft, publishing your book, or receiving your first review. These moments are worth savoring.

Overcoming Challenges

The road to self-publishing is filled with obstacles, but each challenge you overcome adds to the sense of satisfaction you'll feel.

9. Persistence Pays Off

Writing a book, editing it, and navigating the publishing process is no small feat. The determination required to see it through is something to be proud of.

Example: Amanda Hocking faced numerous rejections from traditional publishers before self-publishing her first book. Her persistence led to over a million e-book sales and a lucrative traditional publishing deal.

10. Learning New Skills

As an indie author, you'll gain expertise in areas beyond writing, from marketing to cover design. Each new skill you master is a step toward becoming a well-rounded professional.

Action Step: Reflect on how far you've come. What skills have you developed? What challenges have you overcome? Acknowledge your growth and use it as motivation to keep pushing forward.

Connecting with Readers

One of the most rewarding aspects of self-publishing is the direct connection you can build with your audience.

11. Making an Impact

Your words have the power to entertain, inspire, or change lives. Hearing from readers who were moved by your work is one of the greatest rewards of being an author.

Example: Romance author Colleen Hoover receives countless messages from readers who say her books helped them through difficult times. This connection fuels her passion for writing.

12. Building a Community

Your readers aren't just fans—they're part of your journey. Engaging with them through social media, newsletters, or events creates a sense of shared experience.

> **Pro Tip**: When readers reach out with positive feedback, respond personally whenever possible. These interactions deepen the bond between you and your audience.

The Satisfaction of Owning Your Success

As an indie author, every achievement is a direct result of your efforts. From the first sale to a glowing review, these victories are uniquely yours.

13. Financial Independence

Earning income from your creative work is incredibly satisfying. Even modest success can provide a sense of validation and freedom.

> **Case Study**: Michael J. Sullivan transitioned from indie to hybrid publishing, using his indie success as leverage to negotiate favorable contracts. The financial independence he gained as an indie author allowed him to make decisions on his own terms.

14. Leaving a Legacy

Your books are a lasting contribution to the world. Whether you write fiction that transports readers to another world or non-fiction that educates and inspires, your work has enduring value.

> **Action Step**: Reflect on what your books mean to you and your readers. What legacy do you hope to leave through your writing?

The Indie Author Advantage

Balancing Passion and Professionalism

While personal satisfaction is a powerful motivator, it's important to balance your passion for writing with the realities of running an author business. Here's how to stay motivated without burning out:

1. Set Achievable Goals

Break your larger goals into manageable milestones. Celebrate each achievement to stay energized and focused.

2. Find Joy in the Process

Don't just focus on the end result. Embrace the journey—the act of writing, the thrill of learning, and the satisfaction of connecting with readers.

3. Take Breaks When Needed

Self-publishing is a marathon, not a sprint. Allow yourself time to recharge so you can return to your work with renewed enthusiasm.

Case Study: Joanna Penn's Journey to Fulfillment

Joanna Penn, author and creator of *The Creative Penn*, exemplifies how indie publishing can bring both professional and personal fulfillment. She writes books she's passionate about, shares her expertise with fellow authors, and has built a career that aligns with her values of creativity and freedom.

Action Steps for Embracing Personal Satisfaction

- **Celebrate Milestones**: Take time to recognize your achievements, big or small.
- **Engage with Readers**: Respond to feedback and appreciate the impact your work has on others.
- **Reflect on Your Journey**: Keep a journal or blog about your experiences to track your growth and remind yourself of your accomplishments.
- **Stay True to Your Passion**: Write the stories you love, and trust that your enthusiasm will resonate with readers.

The journey of an indie author is as fulfilling as it is challenging. By focusing on the joy of creation, celebrating your victories, and building connections with readers, you can find immense personal satisfaction in your work. In the next chapter, we'll explore the importance of celebrating your successes and how doing so can inspire your continued growth as an author

10
Celebrating Success

Success as an indie author isn't just about bestseller lists or six-figure incomes. Every step of your journey, from writing "The End" on your first draft to seeing your book on a reader's shelf, is a victory worth celebrating. Recognizing and honoring your achievements keeps you motivated, reinforces your progress, and helps you appreciate how far you've come.

This chapter explores why celebrating your successes is vital, how to do it meaningfully, and how sharing your victories can inspire both you and others.

Why Celebrating Success Matters
Writing and self-publishing are long, challenging processes, and it's easy to focus only on the next task or milestone. Taking the time to celebrate allows you to:

- **Acknowledge Your Hard Work**: Each accomplishment represents countless hours of effort and determination.

- **Boost Your Confidence**: Success, no matter how small, reinforces your ability to achieve your goals.

- **Maintain Motivation**: Celebrating creates positive momentum that propels you forward.
Pro Tip: Don't wait for a "big win" to celebrate. Every step forward—finishing a draft, learning a new skill, or getting your first review—is worth recognizing.

Milestones to Celebrate

As an indie author, your journey is filled with milestones that deserve recognition. Here are a few examples:

1. Writing Milestones
- Completing your first draft.
- Reaching a specific word count.
- Overcoming writer's block to finish a difficult chapter.

2. Publishing Milestones
- Holding your first proof copy.
- Hitting "Publish" on your first book.
- Seeing your book listed on a major platform like Amazon or Barnes & Noble.

3. Sales and Reviews
- Your first sale, no matter how small.
- Receiving your first positive review.
- Reaching a specific sales goal, like 100 copies sold.

Example: An indie fantasy author celebrates their 50th review by hosting a virtual book club where they discuss their favorite fan comments and answer reader questions.

How to Celebrate Your Success

Celebrations don't need to be extravagant to be meaningful. The key is to make them personal and rewarding.

1. Treat Yourself

Reward yourself with something special, like a meal at your favorite restaurant, a small gift, or even a day off to relax.

Pro Tip: Tie your rewards to specific milestones. For example, celebrate completing a draft with a new notebook or pen to inspire your next project.

2. Share Your Success
Letting others in on your achievements can make them feel even more significant. Share your milestones with friends, family, and readers.

Example: Post a photo of your book's first review on social media with a heartfelt thank-you to your readers for their support.

3. Host a Celebration
Mark major milestones, like a book launch or bestseller status, with an event. Options include:
- A virtual book launch party with giveaways.
- A live Q&A session on social media to discuss your journey.

Pro Tip: Use these celebrations as opportunities to engage with your readers and deepen their connection to you.

Inspiring Others Through Your Success
Your wins don't just belong to you—they can inspire other writers and readers. Sharing your journey, including both successes and challenges, creates a sense of community and encourages others to pursue their own goals.

1. Be Honest About the Process
Success is rarely a straight line. Sharing the ups and downs of your journey makes your achievements more relatable and inspiring.

Example: Author Bella Forrest often shares stories about her early struggles and how persistence led to her success. This transparency has motivated countless aspiring authors.

2. Celebrate Readers, Too
Readers are part of your journey. Acknowledge their role in your success by thanking them publicly or creating events that involve them.

Action Step: Consider hosting a "reader appreciation day" where you give away signed copies or exclusive content as a thank-you.

Case Study: Amanda Hocking's Early Wins
Amanda Hocking celebrated her first 1,000 e-book sales by treating herself to a new writing desk. As her success grew, she made a habit of reflecting on her milestones and sharing them with her fans, creating a loyal following that amplified her journey.

Action Steps for Celebrating Success
- **Define Your Milestones**: Write down specific goals you want to celebrate, from completing drafts to hitting sales targets.
- **Plan Your Celebrations**: Decide how you'll reward yourself for each milestone, whether it's a treat, an event, or a shout-out on social media.
- **Share the Joy**: Involve your readers and fellow authors in your celebrations to build deeper connections.
- **Reflect on Your Achievements**: Take time to appreciate how far you've come and how much you've grown as an author.

Celebrating your success is about more than marking achievements—it's about recognizing the value of your hard work, staying motivated, and inspiring others. In the next chapter, we'll explore the importance of retaining ownership of your work and how it empowers you as an indie author.

11
Ownership of Rights

One of the most powerful advantages of independent publishing is retaining full ownership of your work. In traditional publishing, authors often give up significant rights to their manuscripts in exchange for distribution, marketing, and other services. As an indie author, you maintain complete control over your intellectual property, ensuring that you reap the long-term creative and financial benefits.

This chapter explores the importance of ownership, how to protect your rights, and the opportunities that come with being in full control of your work.

The Value of Owning Your Rights
Retaining ownership of your book rights means that you decide how your work is published, distributed, and monetized. Here's why that matters:

1. Long-Term Income
When you own your rights, you retain the ability to profit from your work indefinitely. Even years after publication, your book can continue to generate income, especially if you release new editions or adapt it into other formats.

> **Example**: Hugh Howey's *Wool* series became a bestseller years after its initial release. Because he retained the rights, Howey continues to earn royalties from e-books, print editions, and international translations.

2. Creative Freedom

Owning your rights gives you full control over how your book is represented. From cover design to marketing strategies, you make the decisions that best align with your vision.

> **Pro Tip**: Traditional publishers may ask for changes to make your book more marketable. As an indie author, you can decide whether to make those changes or stay true to your original concept.

3. Opportunities for Adaptation

With full rights ownership, you can explore new opportunities like audiobooks, translations, or even film and TV adaptations. Each format opens up additional revenue streams and audiences.

> **Case Study**: Andy Weir self-published *The Martian* and retained full ownership of his rights. After the book gained popularity, he negotiated deals for print publication and a major motion picture adaptation—on terms favorable to him.

Types of Rights You Own

Understanding the different types of rights you own as an indie author is essential for protecting and monetizing your work effectively.

1. Digital Rights

These cover e-books and other electronic formats. Retaining digital rights is crucial, as e-books often represent the largest source of income for indie authors.

2. Print Rights

Print rights allow you to produce physical copies of your book. Print-on-demand services like Amazon KDP and IngramSpark make it easy to retain control while offering global distribution.

The Indie Author Advantage

3. Audio Rights
Audiobooks are one of the fastest-growing segments in publishing. By retaining your audio rights, you can work with platforms like ACX or Findaway Voices to produce and distribute audiobooks.

4. Translation and Foreign Rights
If your book gains traction, translating it into other languages can open up international markets. Platforms like Babelcube or working directly with translators can help you retain these rights while reaching a global audience.

5. Film and TV Rights
These rights cover adaptations of your work for the screen. If you retain them, you have the freedom to negotiate deals directly, ensuring that your story is represented the way you want.

Protecting Your Rights
Owning your rights is only valuable if you protect them. Here's how to safeguard your intellectual property:

1. Register Your Copyright
In most countries, your work is automatically protected by copyright once it's in a tangible form. However, registering your copyright with the relevant authority provides additional legal protection.
> **Action Step**: In the U.S., register your copyright with the U.S. Copyright Office. This can be done online and is relatively inexpensive.

2. Read Contracts Carefully
If you collaborate with editors, designers, or distributors, ensure their contracts don't inadvertently transfer rights to them.
> **Pro Tip**: Look for "work for hire" clauses in contracts. These ensure that any work created by freelancers remains your property.

3. Use Digital Rights Management (DRM)
DRM tools can help prevent unauthorized distribution of your e-books. While not foolproof, they add an extra layer of protection.
> **Example**: Platforms like Amazon KDP allow you to enable DRM when uploading your book to protect it from being copied or shared without permission.

Monetizing Your Rights
Owning your rights opens up opportunities to monetize your work in multiple ways:

1. Licensing Deals
You can license your book for specific uses—such as foreign translations or print editions—while retaining ownership. Licensing lets you earn income without giving up your rights entirely.
> **Example**: If your book is popular in English-speaking markets, you might license the translation rights to a publisher in Germany for a fixed fee or royalty share.

2. Special Editions
Create premium editions of your book, such as hardcover versions or collector's editions with bonus content. These appeal to dedicated fans and can generate additional income.
> **Action Step**: Use platforms like IngramSpark to produce high-quality hardcover editions and market them directly to your audience.

3. Adaptations
Explore opportunities for adapting your work into new formats. Audiobooks, graphic novels, and even video games can expand your audience and revenue.
> **Case Study: J.K. Rowling and Rights Retention**
> When J.K. Rowling negotiated her publishing deal for *Harry Potter*, she retained e-book rights—a forward-thinking decision at the time. Years later, she launched

her own platform, Pottermore, to sell digital editions and keep a larger share of the profits.

Action Steps for Managing Your Rights
1. **Understand Your Rights**: Familiarize yourself with the different types of rights you own.
2. **Register Your Copyright**: Protect your work by registering it with the appropriate authority.
3. **Review Agreements Carefully**: Ensure contracts with freelancers and distributors don't transfer rights inadvertently.
4. **Explore Licensing Opportunities**: Negotiate deals for translations, print editions, or adaptations while retaining ownership.
5. **Experiment with Formats**: Offer audiobooks, print editions, and other versions of your book to maximize revenue.

Owning your rights is one of the greatest advantages of independent publishing. By understanding and protecting your intellectual property, you empower yourself to create, distribute, and profit from your work on your own terms. In the next chapter, we'll explore how to sustain your writing career by focusing on productivity, consistency, and long-term growth.

12
Building Sustainability

A successful writing career isn't built on a single bestseller—it's sustained through consistent output, smart planning, and adaptability. As an indie author, creating a long-term strategy ensures that you can keep writing, publishing, and connecting with readers for years to come.

This chapter delves into the strategies and habits that will help you build a sustainable author career, from managing your workload to planning for financial stability and creative longevity.

Why Sustainability Matters
Writing is a marathon, not a sprint. Many authors burn out by pushing too hard or neglecting the foundational systems that support their work. Sustainability allows you to:
- **Maintain Creativity**: Avoid burnout and keep your passion for storytelling alive.
- **Build a Loyal Audience**: Readers crave consistency. Regular releases strengthen their trust in you.
- **Achieve Financial Stability**: A steady income lets you focus more on your writing and less on external pressures.

Pro Tip: Think of sustainability as a balance between creative fulfillment, financial growth, and personal well-being.

Establishing a Writing Routine
Consistency is the key to productivity. By developing a writing routine that works for you, you can ensure steady progress without overwhelming yourself.

The Indie Author Advantage

1. Find Your Optimal Writing Time
Identify when you're most creative and focused. For some, it's early morning before the day begins; for others, it's late at night. **Action Step**: Experiment with different schedules for two weeks, tracking your productivity. Use the results to craft a routine tailored to your natural rhythms.

2. Set Realistic Goals
Unrealistic expectations lead to stress and frustration. Instead, set achievable goals for daily word counts, weekly progress, or monthly milestones.
> **Example**: Aim to write 500 words a day if you're starting out. This small, consistent effort can result in a full-length novel in six months.

3. Break Down Big Projects
Dividing your book into manageable sections—such as chapters or scenes—makes the process feel less daunting.
> **Pro Tip**: Use tools like Scrivener or Notion to organize your writing into smaller tasks and track your progress.

Planning Your Releases
A steady publishing schedule keeps your readers engaged and strengthens your presence in the market.

1. Develop a Release Calendar
Plan your book releases for the year, including time for writing, editing, and marketing.
> **Example**: A romance author might aim to release three books a year, with 4 months allocated to each project.

2. Capitalize on Series Momentum
Series are a cornerstone of many successful indie careers. They keep readers coming back for more and increase your chances of cross-selling.

Action Step: Release books in a series at regular intervals, ideally 3–6 months apart, to maintain reader interest.

3. Plan Promotions Strategically

Coordinate sales, discounts, and advertising campaigns around your release calendar to maximize visibility and sales.

Pro Tip: Tie promotions to seasonal events or genre-specific holidays (e.g., spooky sales for Halloween if you write horror).

Diversifying Your Revenue Streams

Relying solely on e-book sales can be risky. Diversifying your income ensures stability and opens up new opportunities.

1. Explore Multiple Formats

Expand your offerings to include print books, audiobooks, and box sets.

Example: Lindsay Buroker maximizes her income by selling e-books, paperbacks, and audiobooks while regularly bundling her series into box sets for promotional sales.

2. Monetize Your Expertise

If you've mastered the self-publishing process, consider sharing your knowledge through workshops, coaching, or online courses.

Case Study: Mark Dawson, a successful indie thriller author, created an online course to teach other authors about advertising and marketing, adding a lucrative income stream to his career.

3. Consider Subscription Models

Platforms like Patreon allow you to earn recurring income by offering exclusive content, such as bonus stories, writing insights, or sneak peeks.

> **Action Step**: Start small by offering two or three reward tiers on Patreon and build your subscriber base gradually.

Financial Planning for Longevity

Managing your finances wisely is crucial for a sustainable career.

1. Budget for Your Career

Set aside a portion of your earnings for professional expenses like editing, cover design, and marketing. Treat your writing as a business.

> **Action Step**: Use tools like QuickBooks or Wave to track your income and expenses.

2. Build an Emergency Fund

Publishing trends and personal circumstances can change unexpectedly. Having a financial cushion ensures you can weather slow periods.

> **Pro Tip**: Aim to save 3–6 months of living expenses as a safety net.

3. Reinvest in Your Growth

Use part of your earnings to invest in tools, training, or marketing strategies that can elevate your career.

> **Example**: Reinvesting royalties into Amazon Ads or a professional website redesign can pay off in increased visibility and sales.

Maintaining Creative Energy

Burnout is a real risk for indie authors. Prioritizing your mental and creative health is essential for long-term success.

1. Take Breaks

Schedule downtime between projects to recharge and avoid creative fatigue.

Pro Tip: Use breaks to read widely, explore hobbies, or take a vacation. Inspiration often strikes when you're not actively writing.

2. Mix Up Your Projects

Switching between genres, formats, or writing styles can keep your creativity fresh.

Example: An author who primarily writes thrillers might experiment with a short romantic suspense story to explore new ideas and skills.

3. Stay Connected to Your "Why"

Remind yourself why you started writing. Whether it's to tell stories that matter, entertain readers, or achieve personal goals, reconnecting with your purpose can reignite your passion.

Case Study: Bella Andre's Steady Growth
Romance author Bella Andre built her career on sustainable practices. By consistently releasing books, diversifying her formats, and engaging with her readers, she turned her passion into a thriving, long-term business.

Action Steps for Building Sustainability

1. **Create a Routine**: Develop a writing schedule that fits your lifestyle and energy levels.
2. **Plan Ahead**: Map out a release calendar and coordinate your writing and marketing efforts.
3. **Diversify Income**: Explore multiple revenue streams, from audiobooks to courses.
4. **Manage Finances Wisely**: Budget for expenses, build an emergency fund, and reinvest in your career.
5. **Prioritize Self-Care**: Take breaks, mix up your projects, and focus on maintaining your creative energy.

Sustainability isn't just about financial success—it's about creating a fulfilling career that aligns with your goals and passions. In the next chapter, we'll explore how to build a legacy

The Indie Author Advantage

by making a lasting impact on your readers and the literary world.

13
Building a Legacy

Writing and publishing your books is about more than sales or accolades—it's about leaving a lasting impression. Whether through stories that touch readers' hearts, non-fiction that informs and inspires, or a creative journey that serves as a beacon for others, indie authors have the opportunity to create a meaningful legacy.

This chapter explores how to build a literary and personal legacy that resonates with readers, supports other authors, and leaves a positive impact on the publishing world.

What Does It Mean to Build a Legacy?
A legacy is the enduring influence of your work and contributions. For an indie author, it encompasses:
- **Your Books**: The stories or ideas you've shared with the world.
- **Your Impact on Readers**: How your work has entertained, educated, or inspired.
- **Your Role in the Community**: Contributions to fellow authors and the broader literary ecosystem.

Pro Tip: A legacy is built over time. Focus on authenticity and purpose, and let the results follow naturally.

Writing Books That Last
Crafting a legacy begins with your writing. By focusing on quality and relevance, you can create books that resonate for years to come.

The Indie Author Advantage

1. Write with Meaning

Consider what you want readers to take away from your work. Whether it's a sense of wonder, a fresh perspective, or practical advice, books that make an emotional or intellectual impact endure.

> **Example**: Harper Lee's *To Kill a Mockingbird* remains relevant decades later because of its timeless exploration of morality, empathy, and justice.

2. Focus on Quality

Invest in professional editing, cover design, and formatting to ensure your books meet the highest standards. A well-crafted book is more likely to stand the test of time.

3. Diversify Your Catalog

Building a diverse body of work increases your chances of connecting with readers across generations and interests. Consider expanding into new genres, formats, or themes as your career progresses.

> **Example**: Neil Gaiman's range—from fantasy novels to children's books and graphic novels—has made his work accessible and beloved by multiple audiences.

Connecting with Readers

A true legacy is built not just on what you create, but on how it affects others. Building strong relationships with your readers ensures that your work remains cherished.

4. Engage Authentically

Interact with readers through social media, email newsletters, and events. Share your journey, respond to feedback, and let your readers feel connected to you.

> **Pro Tip**: Consider hosting virtual Q&A sessions or writing workshops to deepen your bond with your audience.

2. Empower Your Readers

Encourage readers to share their experiences with your books. Whether through reviews, fan art, or word of mouth, reader engagement amplifies your legacy.

> **Example**: Fantasy author Sarah J. Maas has cultivated a devoted fanbase by actively interacting with readers, inspiring fan art and online discussions that keep her work alive in the cultural conversation.

3. Write for Future Generations

Think about how your work will be received years from now. Avoid relying too heavily on trends, and aim for universal themes and timeless characters.

Mentoring and Supporting Other Authors

Part of your legacy can be the role you play in lifting up other writers. Sharing your knowledge and offering guidance strengthens the indie community as a whole.

1. Share Your Knowledge

Write blog posts, record podcasts, or create courses to help aspiring authors navigate the publishing process.

> **Case Study**: Joanna Penn's *The Creative Penn* podcast has helped thousands of indie authors by providing practical advice and inspiration.

2. Collaborate with Emerging Writers

Offer opportunities for co-authoring or include new voices in anthologies. Collaboration benefits everyone involved and fosters goodwill.

3. Champion Diversity and Inclusion

Support authors from underrepresented backgrounds by amplifying their voices, offering mentorship, or collaborating on projects that celebrate diverse perspectives.

> **Pro Tip**: Use your platform to highlight books or authors that align with your values.

The Indie Author Advantage

Preserving Your Work
Ensuring your books remain available and accessible is key to building a legacy that endures.

1. Maintain Your Rights
By retaining ownership of your rights (as discussed in Chapter 11), you ensure that your work remains in your control for future adaptations, reprints, or updates.

2. Keep Your Backlist Active
Even as you release new books, regularly promote your older titles. A strong backlist can generate consistent sales and maintain your presence in the market.
> **Action Step**: Periodically refresh your backlist with updated covers or bonus content to attract new readers.

3. Archive Your Process
Document your journey through blogs, newsletters, or journals. These records not only preserve your insights for future authors but also provide material for memoirs or writing guides.
> **Example**: Anne Lamott's *Bird by Bird* has inspired generations of writers by offering a candid look at the creative process.

Giving Back to the Indie Community
Supporting the next wave of indie authors ensures the continued growth and success of self-publishing.

1. Host Workshops and Events
Organize writing retreats, webinars, or local meetups to share your expertise and build connections.

2. Advocate for Indie Authors
Use your platform to highlight the achievements of other self-published writers and promote the value of independent publishing.

Example: Author David Gaughran is a vocal advocate for indie authors, regularly sharing resources and insights through his blog and books.

3. Leave a Legacy of Generosity

Your willingness to help others, share knowledge, and celebrate success can inspire countless authors to follow your example.

Case Study: Hugh Howey's Lasting Influence

Hugh Howey not only achieved success with his *Wool* series but also used his platform to support other indie authors. By sharing his journey and advocating for the rights of self-published writers, he has left a lasting impact on the indie publishing world.

Action Steps for Building Your Legacy

1. **Define Your Vision**: Reflect on the message and impact you want to leave behind.
2. **Focus on Quality**: Invest in crafting books that readers will treasure for years.
3. **Engage with Readers**: Build authentic connections and encourage their participation.
4. **Support Other Authors**: Share your knowledge, collaborate, and advocate for diversity in publishing.
5. **Preserve Your Work**: Keep your backlist active and document your journey for future generations.

Your legacy is the mark you leave on the world through your words, actions, and connections. By focusing on authenticity, quality, and community, you can create a body of work—and a reputation—that inspires readers and writers alike. In the final chapter, we'll bring everything together, focusing on how to celebrate and grow as an indie author while looking toward the future.

14
The Indie Author's Journey Forward

Becoming an indie author is not just a career choice—it's a journey of self-expression, resilience, and growth. From crafting compelling stories to navigating the complexities of publishing, every step you take builds your skills, strengthens your resolve, and shapes your identity as a creator. While this book has provided strategies, tools, and insights for your success, the journey ahead is yours to define.

This final chapter explores how to continue thriving as an indie author, grow your career, and embrace the opportunities and challenges of the ever-evolving publishing world.

Reflecting on Your Accomplishments
The first step to moving forward is recognizing how far you've come. Whether you've published multiple books or are preparing to release your first, take pride in what you've achieved.

1. Celebrate Your Growth
Look back at your journey so far. Reflect on the skills you've gained, the obstacles you've overcome, and the connections you've built.

> **Exercise**: Write down three specific milestones you're proud of—big or small. These could include finishing your first draft, publishing a book, or receiving heartfelt feedback from a reader.

2. Embrace Your Unique Path

No two indie authors' journeys are the same. Your successes, struggles, and triumphs are part of what make your story compelling. Use these experiences to fuel your future growth.

> **Pro Tip**: Remember that comparing your progress to others can be unproductive. Focus instead on how you've evolved as an author and what you want to achieve next.

Setting Your Next Goals

With each milestone comes the opportunity to set new, ambitious goals. Defining your vision for the future keeps you motivated and ensures continued growth.

1. Identify Long-Term Goals

Think about where you'd like to be in five or ten years. Do you want to write in new genres, build a backlist of 20 books, or hit a specific income target? Long-term goals give you a clear sense of direction.

> **Example**: A mystery author might set a goal of writing three interconnected series over the next decade, with plans for spin-offs or adaptations.

2. Break Goals into Manageable Steps

Large goals can feel overwhelming, but breaking them into smaller tasks makes them achievable. For example:

- **Goal**: Publish a series of five books.
- **Steps**: Outline the series, write the first book, hire a cover designer, and launch the first title with a marketing plan.

3. Stay Flexible

The publishing world is unpredictable, and your interests may evolve. Allow room for adjustments to your goals as you grow and as the market changes.

> **Pro Tip**: Revisit your goals annually to assess your progress and make updates based on new opportunities or challenges.

Continuing Your Education
The best indie authors are lifelong learners. Staying informed about trends, technologies, and best practices ensures that your strategies remain effective.

1. Follow Industry Leaders
Stay updated by following blogs, podcasts, and newsletters from experts like Joanna Penn, David Gaughran, and Mark Dawson.

2. Attend Workshops and Conferences
Live events—whether in-person or virtual—are invaluable for networking and learning. Take advantage of opportunities to connect with peers and gain new insights.

> **Example**: Participate in an online summit focused on Amazon Ads or audiobook production to refine your skills in those areas.

3. Experiment with New Tools
Publishing technologies are always evolving. Embrace new tools and platforms to streamline your processes, reach more readers, and enhance your work.

> **Action Step**: Test one new tool or technique every six months, such as a social media scheduler, advanced formatting software, or a new advertising platform.

Embracing Challenges and Growth
Every indie author faces setbacks, from slow sales to creative slumps. The key to long-term success is viewing challenges as opportunities for growth.

1. Learn from Mistakes
Publishing a book that underperforms or receiving harsh criticism can be discouraging, but it's also a chance to improve.

Analyze what went wrong, and use those lessons to refine your approach.

> **Example**: If a launch fails to gain traction, consider whether pricing, marketing, or genre expectations played a role, and adjust for your next release.

2. Take Creative Risks

Pushing yourself out of your comfort zone can lead to breakthroughs. Try writing in a new genre, experimenting with serialized fiction, or co-authoring with another writer.

3. Celebrate Persistence

Sometimes, success takes longer than expected. Remember that every step forward, no matter how small, brings you closer to your goals.

> **Pro Tip**: Keep a "success journal" where you record your wins—such as finishing a chapter, receiving a great review, or hitting a sales milestone. This can be a powerful motivator during challenging times.

Looking to the Future of Publishing

The indie publishing industry is constantly evolving, and staying adaptable is essential for continued success. Here are some trends to watch:

1. Growth of Audiobooks

Audiobooks are one of the fastest-growing segments in publishing. If you haven't explored this format yet, now might be the time.

2. Rise of Subscription Models

Platforms like Kindle Unlimited and Scribd continue to shape how readers consume books. Understanding these models can help you adapt your strategies.

The Indie Author Advantage

3. Global Markets
The international market for e-books is expanding rapidly. Translating your work or distributing to new regions can open up exciting opportunities.
> **Action Step**: Research translation platforms like Babelcube or Reedsy, and explore global distribution options through Draft2Digital or IngramSpark.

Leaving a Mark
Your journey as an indie author is part of a larger movement that's transforming the publishing world. By staying true to your voice, supporting other authors, and connecting with readers, you're helping to shape the future of storytelling.

1. Inspire Others
Share your experiences to encourage aspiring authors. Your successes and lessons learned can motivate others to take the leap into indie publishing.

2. Be a Champion for Change
Advocate for diversity, innovation, and inclusion in publishing. Use your platform to amplify underrepresented voices and contribute to a thriving creative community.

Action Steps for Moving Forward
1. **Reflect**: Acknowledge your achievements and take pride in your progress.
2. **Plan**: Set new, actionable goals that align with your vision.
3. **Learn**: Stay informed about industry trends and embrace new tools and techniques.
4. **Adapt**: View challenges as opportunities for growth, and stay open to change.
5. **Inspire**: Share your journey to support and uplift the indie author community.

A Final Word

The indie author path is not always easy, but it's one of the most rewarding journeys you can take. By embracing your creativity, learning from your experiences, and staying connected to your readers, you can build a career—and a legacy—that you're proud of.

Your next chapter begins now. Go forth and write your story.

About the Author

B Alan Bourgeois began his writing journey at age 12, crafting screenplays for *Adam-12* as an outlet to develop his style. While he never submitted these works, the experience fueled his passion for storytelling. After following the conventional advice of pursuing a stable career, Bourgeois rediscovered his love for writing in 1989 through a community college class, leading to his first published short story. Since then, he has written over 48 short stories, published more than 10 books, including the award-winning *Extinguishing the Light*, and made his mark in the publishing world.

Recognizing the challenges authors face, Bourgeois founded Creative House Press in the early 2000s, publishing 60 books by other authors in five years and gaining insights into the industry's marketing needs. In 2011, he launched the Texas Authors Association, which grew to include two nonprofits promoting Texas writers and literacy. He also created innovative programs like the Lone Star Festival and short story contests for students, and in 2016, the Authors Marketing Event, offering a groundbreaking Certification program for book marketing expertise.

Despite setbacks during the COVID-19 pandemic, Bourgeois adapted by launching the Authors School of Business, providing essential tools for authors to succeed as "Authorpreneurs." As publishing evolves, he has explored NFTs as a potential revenue stream for writers. With decades of experience, Bourgeois remains a driving force in the literary community, committed to helping authors thrive in a changing industry.

Bourgeois is currently the director of the Texas Authors Museum & Institute of History, based in Austin, Texas

Other Books by the Author in this Series

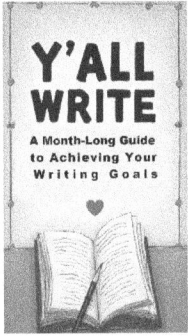

Y'all Write: A Month-Long Guide to Achieving Your Writing Goals

Unlock your creative potential with *Y'all Write: A Month of Writing Celebration and Growth*! This guide offers tips, motivation, and tools to help writers of all levels set goals, build momentum, and embrace the joy of storytelling.

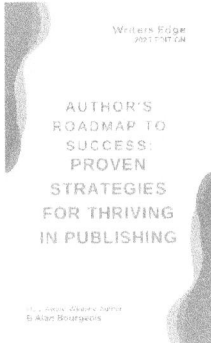

Author's Roadmap to Success: Proven Strategies for Thriving in Publishing

Unlock the secrets to literary success with *Author's Roadmap to Success: Proven Strategies for Thriving in Publishing*. This essential guide provides actionable strategies to help writers build strong habits, master self-publishing, and thrive in their writing careers.

The Writer's Self-Care Guide: Top Ten Steps to Balance and Thrive

Transform your writing journey with *The Writer's Self-Care Guide: Top Ten Steps to Balance and Thrive*. This practical guide offers actionable steps to nurture your creativity, set boundaries, and achieve a balanced, fulfilling writing life.

The Indie Author Advantage

Top Ten Keys for Successful Writing and Productivity

Unlock your writing potential with *Top Ten Keys for Successful Writing and Productivity*. This guide offers actionable strategies to build consistent habits, manage time effectively, and produce high-quality work to elevate your writing

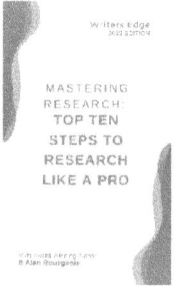

Mastering Research: Top Ten Steps to Research Like a Pro

Elevate your writing with *Mastering Research: Top Ten Steps to Research Like a Pro*. This essential guide provides practical tools and techniques to conduct thorough, credible research and seamlessly integrate it into your work.

Character Chronicles: Crafting Depth and Consistency in Creative Projects

Bring your characters to life with *Character Chronicles: Crafting Depth and Consistency in Creative Projects*. This essential guide reveals professional techniques to develop authentic, complex characters that resonate across any creative medium.

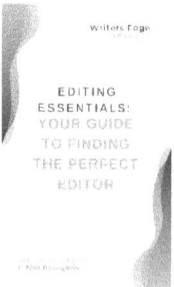

Editing Essentials: Your Guide to Finding the Perfect Editor

Transform your manuscript with *Editing Essentials: Your Guide to Finding the Perfect Editor*. This guide provides practical steps to identify, evaluate, and collaborate with the ideal editor to elevate your writing.

AI Programs Apps Authors Should Use

Revolutionize your writing with *Top Ten AI Programs Authors Should Use*. This guide explores powerful AI tools like Grammarly and Scrivener, offering practical tips to enhance creativity, productivity, and efficiency.

The Business of Writing

Master the publishing world with *Unlocking the Business of Writing*. This essential guide provides expert advice and practical tips to build your author platform, maximize royalties, and turn your passion into a thriving career.

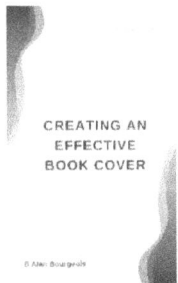

Creating an Effective Book Cover

Create a book cover that captivates readers with *Top Ten Keys to Creating an Effective Book Cover*. This guide offers expert tips and practical advice on design, branding, and marketing to make your book stand out.

Mastering the Art of the Sales Pitch

Master the art of the sales pitch with *Mastering the Art of the Sales Pitch*. This guide provides essential strategies to captivate your audience, highlight your book's value, and drive its success.

The Indie Author Advantage

Publishing Issues Authors Deal With

Overcome publishing challenges with *Publishing Issues Authors Deal With*. This guide offers practical strategies and expert insights to help you navigate rejection, editing, marketing, and more to achieve your publishing dreams.

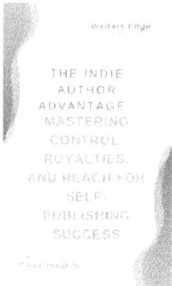

The Indie Author Advantage: Mastering Control, Royalties, and Reach for Self-Publishing Success

Thrive as an indie author with *The Indie Author Advantage: Mastering Control, Royalties, and Reach for Self-Publishing Success*. This guide offers actionable strategies to retain creative control, maximize royalties, and reach a global audience.

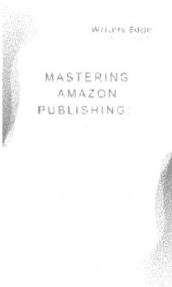

Mastering Amazon Publishing: A Comprehensive Guide to Success for Indie Authors

Achieve self-publishing success with *Mastering Amazon Publishing: A Comprehensive Guide to Success for Indie Authors*. This guide provides proven strategies to navigate KDP, boost visibility, and maximize earnings for your books.

Marketing Essentials for Authors: Proven Strategies to Boost Book Sales

Boost your book sales with *Top Ten Marketing Essentials for Authors: Proven Strategies to Promote Your Book*. This guide combines traditional and digital marketing tactics to help authors effectively connect with readers and turn their books into bestsellers.

Marketing Mastery: Avoiding Common Mistakes for Authors

Master book marketing with *Marketing Mastery: Avoiding Common Mistakes for Authors*. This guide offers actionable advice to help authors connect with readers, build a strong online presence, and achieve their publishing goals.

The Author Branding Blueprint

Elevate your writing career with *Author Brand Mastery: A Comprehensive Guide to Building and Sustaining Your Unique Identity*. This guide provides practical steps to define your brand, build a professional presence, and connect meaningfully with your audience.

Reader Magnet: Top Strategies for Building an Engaged Reader Community

Build a loyal reader community with *Reader Magnet: Top Strategies for Building an Engaged Reader Community*. This guide offers actionable strategies to connect with readers, create exclusive content, and turn your audience into passionate advocates.

The Indie Author Advantage

Author Platform Mastery: A Comprehensive Guide to Building, Monetizing, and Growing Your Audience

Build your literary empire with *Author Platform Mastery: A Comprehensive Guide to Building, Monetizing, and Growing Your Audience*. This essential guide offers practical strategies to define your brand, engage readers, and expand your reach.

Networking Success for Authors: Essential Strategies Guide

Achieve your literary goals with *Networking Success for Authors: Essential Strategies Guide*. This practical roadmap offers strategies to build meaningful connections, promote your work, and create a supportive community for lasting success.

Write, Publish, Market: The Ultimate Handbook for Author Success
ISBN:

Master the modern publishing landscape with *Write, Publish, Market: The Ultimate Handbook for Author Success*. This guide provides actionable strategies to build your author brand, attract readers, and achieve long-term success in your writing career.

Mastering Interviews: Essential Tips for Authors' Success

Excel in interviews with *Mastering Interviews: Essential Tips for Authors' Success*. This guide offers practical advice to confidently promote your work, connect with audiences, and turn every interview into a memorable success.

Mastering Event Presentations: Avoiding Common Author Mistakes

Captivate your audience with *Mastering Event Presentations: Avoiding Common Author Mistakes*. This guide offers practical strategies to avoid pitfalls, engage your audience, and deliver impactful presentations that boost your confidence and connect with readers.

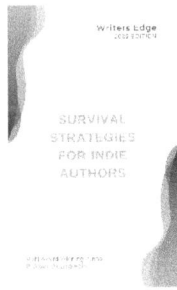

Survival Strategies for Indie Authors: Overcoming Challenges and Achieving Success

Thrive as an indie author with *Survival Strategies for Indie Authors: Overcoming Challenges and Achieving Success*. This guide provides practical advice and actionable tips to overcome obstacles, enhance your skills, and achieve your publishing goals.

The Indie Author Advantage

Empowering Authors: Top Ten Strategies for Writing Success and Career Growth

Achieve your writing dreams with *Empowering Authors: Top Ten Strategies for Writing Success and Career Growth*. This guide offers practical advice and proven strategies to build habits, refine your craft, and grow your author career with confidence.

The Sacred Connection

Infuse your writing with mindfulness and purpose through *Creating with Spirit: The Sacred Art of Writing and Publishing*. This guide transforms your creative journey into a spiritual practice, empowering you to inspire readers and overcome challenges with authenticity and intention.

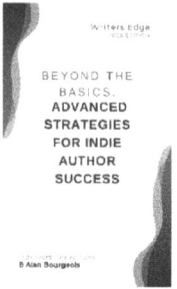

Beyond the Basics: Advanced Strategies for Indie Author Success
ISBN:

Elevate your indie publishing career with *Beyond the Basics: Advanced Strategies for Indie Author Success*. This guide offers actionable tips and strategies to diversify income, engage readers, and build a sustainable, thriving career.

The AI Author: Embracing the Future of Fiction

Embrace the future of storytelling with *The AI Author: Balancing Efficiency and Creativity in Fiction Writing*. This guide helps authors harness AI to boost productivity and creativity while preserving the emotional depth and artistry of creating.

The Non-Fiction Nexus: Balancing AI and Human Insight in the Future of Writing

Elevate your non-fiction writing with *The Non-Fiction Nexus: Balancing AI and Human Insight in the Future of Writing*. This guide shows how to harness AI's efficiency while preserving the creativity and ethical judgment that make your work truly impactful.

Authorship Reimagined: NFTs and Blockchain Essentials
ISBN:

Embrace the future of publishing with *NFT and Blockchain Essentials for Authors' Success*. This guide explains how blockchain and NFTs can protect your work, automate royalties, and expand your audience while maximizing revenue.

The Indie Author Advantage

Adapting Success: Your Book's Journey to Film

Turn your book into a cinematic sensation with *From Page to Screen: A Step-by-Step Guide to Adapting Your Book into a Blockbuster Film*. This guide provides practical advice and industry insights to help you navigate the adaptation process and bring your story to life on the big screen.

Beyond the Basics: Advanced Strategies for Indie Author Success

Elevate your indie publishing career with this ultimate guide to mastering advanced strategies in writing, marketing, and global distribution. Packed with actionable tips and real-world examples, it empowers authors to balance creativity with entrepreneurship and build sustainable, thriving careers.

2026: The Ultimate Year for Indie Authors

Make 2026 your breakthrough year with *The Ultimate Year for Indie Authors*. This guide offers practical strategies to optimize publishing, leverage social media, and achieve unparalleled success in your indie author journey.